All Scripture references taken from the KJV
of the Holy Bible, unless otherwise indicated.

ONE DEFINING DAY : *A Day When Dreams Come True*

by Dr. Marlene Miles

Freshwater Press 2026

Freshwaterpress9@gmail.com

ISBN: 978-1-971933-08-5

Paperback Version

Table of Contents

ONE DEFINING DAY

When Dreams Come True

Freshwater

Psalm 126

A song of ascents.

When the Lord restored the fortunes of Zion,
we were like those who dreamed.
Our mouths were filled with laughter,
our tongues with songs of joy.
Then it was said among the nations,
"The Lord has done great things for them."
The Lord has done great things for us,
and we are filled with joy.

Restore our fortunes, Lord,
like streams in the Negev.
Those who sow with tears
will reap with songs of joy.
Those who go out weeping,
carrying seed to sow,
will return with songs of joy,
carrying sheaves with them.

PREFACE

When the LORD restored the fortunes of
Zion, we were like those who dreamed.
(Psalm 126:1)

Flesh is so now. We are so microwave,
laser, AI generation, we want it fast, we want it
now. We don't boss God; we don't change His
timing. Too many are said to find out that it not
only *is what it is* it is **when** God says it is.

Whether we've been waiting a long
time or not, to our flesh, it's been like forever.
I'll give a dental injection that takes 3 seconds.
Most people do not care or notice the injection.
I'll get about one in a hundred who is freaking
out, and I'm done, needle is recapped and back
on the table before they even warm up their
freak out. So, 4 seconds later when they open
their eyes, I ask them, "Does it still hurt?" Then
they realize they've been performing for
nothing and no reason. Most of that 1% will

say, "I didn't even feel it." So, when it's something the flesh wants it takes forever. That is the nature of carnal man; that is the nature of a man whose soul is not yet full prospered. When it is something that the flesh doesn't want, it took too long.

Until reality visits.

I'm reality. I am not God but in that dental setting at that moment, I am reality: "Does it still hurt?"

Of course it doesn't, I'm not even touching you.

And the converse of that, when you finally get that thing you want after you had forgotten how long you wanted it or how long you've been waiting for it—you've even forgotten that you wanted it, asked for it or waited for it, but God, who is God AND reality delivers.

Oh, what a day. O Happy Day, it's like a dream; it's finally here.

INTRODUCTION

There are people whose lives read like a long list of losses. Not dramatic losses that come with sympathy cards and casseroles, but the quieter kind that stretch across decades and never seem to let up.

I have a friend like that.

Her father died when she was only ten years old. Not metaphorically or emotionally, but his heart literally stopped. There was mystery surrounding his death and that only fueled pain and lack of closure, as if it is ever simple to close such a loss. At only 10 years old, something in her life stopped with that devastating first, unexpected, unbalanced loss. Yet, that was the beginning of losses for her.

She married young, to a much older man, who had his own control issues; but she endured. Years later, she buried him. She married again, and that man turned out to be a deceiver, but God brought her through. Loss did not just visit her life; it kept her address. Her mother lived with her — always. In every house. In every season, never leaving. While honoring an aging parent is noble, it is also heavy when it is uninterrupted, unrelieved, and lifelong.

Then there was a terrible incident at the hospital. Something went wrong. And afterward, she lost her voice. Her formerly strong vocals were whittled down to only a husky, breathy whisper as she tried to project as much as possible to just be heard. The same voice that lamented her father, that spent time with and kept her mother company throughout her mother's entire life as a mother, the same voice that mourned her brother who also died early, and then her husband of many years. The same voice that worshipped into the night seasons anyhow and that prayed for the lost and the sick and taught in houses of God and every other setting and proclaimed what 'thus saith the Lord." That was the voice that was taken. It was as though the devil was saying that he could keep doing stuff to her and there was nothing she could do or say about it.

For ten years. Ten solid years. Ten years of trying to be heard without being able to speak the way she once did. Ten years of living muted — externally and, in many ways, internally.

If you were watching her life from the outside, you might wonder is this the last thing? Is this the thing that is too much for her to bear? You might reasonably conclude that this is a tragedy that does not turn around.

Or can it?

But last night, I spoke with her over the phone. As we talked, something hit me all at once.

Her voice is back. Fully back.

I hadn't noticed it gradually. And I hadn't even noticed it at the onset of the conversation because what we were talking about was so joyful that we were both so excited. I hadn't marked the milestones. I only realized it in that moment — listening to her laugh, to speak freely, to sound like herself again, that something had been restored.

Then the rest of it came rushing in.

God had redeemed the time. God had restored the years.

Her mother passed a few years ago. Her long season of caretaking has ended. Without expecting it outwardly, she has been *found* — not by a rescuer, not by a fixer, but by a wonderful human being **her own age**. God has redeemed the time. God has matched her with someone age-appropriate with similar interests and youthful vitality to share those interests. He is not someone she must manage, parent, or outlive because that person's time would come so much sooner than hers and they could not cheat time. God has sent her someone to love and enjoy, in the same season.

This is someone who walks beside her.

She is getting married soon. She is happy. She is having fun. She is alive in a way she has never been allowed to be before. Silly teenage years will be lived. Fun 20-something years, and so on. This is how redeemed time looks to her life. Yet, they are adults who have adult responsibilities that they manage well. But the things she didn't have from earlier in life because they were stolen from her are now being returned, and in spades. These two have God and they have love and they have each other.

This redemption didn't come piece by piece and she didn't have to figure it out or force anything to make it happen. No, it came *all at once*. It is that one defining day when you realize it, when you see it, when you touch it and taste that the Lord is good and He has revealed Himself to you, or to my friend, Miranda.

If you had asked me years ago whether her life would ever read like redemption, I wouldn't have known how to answer honestly.

But here we are.

Only God could have assembled that many restorations into the same season and made them arrive so suddenly, so quietly, so completely. That is what this book is about.

ONE DEFINING DAY

Childhood and adolescence feel slow. Waiting. Waiting for milestones sweet sixteen and other birthdays, driver's license, graduation, adulthood. The wait feels hopeful and endless at the same time. But then, adulthood arrives and things suddenly feel fast. The years seem to compress. Time feels like it slips. In just a few years too many begin to ask, *What happened to the time?*

Looking forward to getting your driver's license as a teenager is when all the 15 and 16-year-olds wait together. After that, you stop waiting *together.* You start waiting privately, individually, separately. *Then,* most things are no longer guaranteed by age alone.

The driver's license can feel like the last real wait. Before adulthood, time is measured by external gates. Age controls access and waiting has a visible end date. "When I'm 16, then..." After that, life becomes non-linear. Outcomes are no longer time-locked. Waiting becomes ambiguous. You're no longer waiting for a date on the calendar. At this point you should be working toward and waiting for *alignment, and t*hat changes how time feels.

Time feels faster afterward for three simple reasons. Novelty slows time; everything before adulthood is new. You start school, get a first crush, new freedom, new responsibilities. New experiences stretch perception. After that, life becomes repetitive. Life falls into routines, patterns and familiarity. The brain compresses familiar experiences, so time doesn't actually speed up, memory does.

Don't panic about days and time; you are not losing time anymore than the next guy. I can kid and say that gravity may be broken because I don't weigh this much, but I cannot say that Time is broken. It is not.

Waiting changes form. Before adulthood you wait for things that will definitely happen. After adulthood, you wait for things that might not--, or you may worry that they might not happen. It all depends on your relationship with God and your faith. Waiting on things such as marriage, purpose, healing, resolution, and restoration feels heavier, making time feel elusive or slippery.

Responsibility collapses time. Children *live in time*. Adults *manage time*. Management compresses experience. You don't *notice* time, you spend it. The last time most people truly waited *without anxiety* was before they understood loss. It was before they understood not really owning much of anything at all; everything belonged to your parents. Depending on what kind of parents you had, they may not let you forget that you don't own anything. They may have let you know that they own everything.

The driver's license finally comes and it's yours, it's really yours; it even has your picture on it. You believe you are about to step into adulthood because you actually have a license. But it also came before there was any grief that your parents didn't protect you from. It came before unanswered prayer—if you had even started to pray yet. It came before bills and prolonged responsibility. After that, waiting becomes vulnerable.

So, by the time God restores something after years of waiting, it feels dreamlike — not just because it came, but because you forgot what uncomplicated waiting felt like.

Getting that driver's license, for example is Psalm 126 in lived form. It seemed to take forever to get old enough to drive. And then suddenly, decades passed. Somewhere along the way, waiting stopped being about age, and started being about God.

The driver's license being the last shared natural wait is so real to so many. You're not in school with your teenage friends anymore when you probably talked about that rite of passage if not every day, then every week. Then you talked about if you'd get a car and what kind of car it might be. That made it feel like it was taking forever because we thought we were ready right then.

We should keep hope alive and somehow hope makes the wait bearable while you wait on your breakthrough. That breakthrough that really proves you're not a kid anymore, you've done all the steps necessary from birth to now: you can turn, crawl, toddle, walk, run and now you are legal to drive, you are really mobile.

Maybe then, or decades later we realize that mobility was the entire goal all along. But where are we going? What is all this mobility *for*?

IT REALLY HAPPENED

The breakthrough did not happen in one day, but when it arrived, the confirmation that God is, that God can, and that God did is evident. One defining day, multiple events, signs, conversations, shifts, and outcomes arrive back-to-back. The effect is unmistakable, *It is done.*

> When the LORD restored the fortunes of Zion, we were like those who dreamed.
> (Psalm 126:1)

This book is about **sudden visibility after long invisibility**.

When I believed that all things were working together for my good and i could see those all things all at once or right after the other, it was no longer about the things, but it was about the faith. It was about God, it was amazing and marvelous that my waiting, my being, my believing, in knowing that my living is not in vain.

Like Hagar in the wilderness. God really sees me. He really sees me. He heard me; He really heard me. He knows me; He really does. He loves me; He really loves me. Amen.

It was not theoretically, not someday. I believed it because I could see those "all things" lining up — *at the same time that recently, I was sure I was having my very fine, defining day.*

There were multiple confirmations, multiple shifts, multiple answers arriving in close succession. The signs were there, the signals were there. It felt like one of those moments Scripture describes so simply it almost sounds unreal.

When the LORD restored the fortunes of Zion, we were like those who dreamed.
(Psalm 126:1)

There are days like that. Days when nothing new actually begins, but everything hidden is suddenly revealed. Days when you realize God did not rush, forget, or abandon the process. No, He finished it.

And then, in a single stretch of time, He lets you **see** it. This book is not about instant miracles. It is about **sudden clarity**. It is about the day when you wake up and realize that your prayer or prayers were heard. That the answer was already formed, and the outcome is no longer theory or only lodged in faith, it has become real, it has loosed itself and it is not only on the way to you, it is nearly in your hands – as touching.

As I write this now, I will tell you the truth: I am not as sure as I once was about my perfect, defining day, but I know that if not now, very soon. The seeming delay is not because God changed, but because seasons do.

This book is for people who have waited longer than they thought they would or could. For those who have carried more than they should have had to, and wondered whether the story they are living will ever resolve into meaning.

It is for those who may not get everything they hoped for, but who, one day, receive enough confirmations at once to know: *It was not wasted. It was not random. And it was not in vain.*

This is a book about the day when dreams come true not because they arrived quickly, but because they did arrive and they also arrived *complete*.

WHY GOD OFTEN WAITS SO LONG

If God is capable of sudden restoration, then the question almost everyone asks — quietly or aloud — is this:

Why the wait?

Why years of silence before a single day of clarity? Why endurance before evidence? Why does God allow a story to look unfinished for so long?

The temptation is to assume delay means denial, disinterest, or indifference by God. it is to assume that God doesn't see you, hear you, or is working on your case. But delay is often none of those things. Delay is usually development.

There are parts of a life that cannot be fixed in pieces. They must be addressed in layers. Those things about you and your life such as identity, capacity, discernment, and strength. Those things that say that your soul is prospering so that the rest of your life will follow suit can have great impact on your defining day.

Miranda did not just lose people. She lost safety. She lost voice. She lost the luxury of being carefree.

Had restoration come early, it would have been partial. Had love come sooner, it might have required her to shrink again. Had joy arrived before she was finished being responsible for everyone else, it would have been interrupted.

God was not just planning an answer, He was planning a **lasting** one. Some seasons stretch because the outcome requires development into maturity you don't yet possess, freedom you don't yet have, or discernment you haven't yet learned.

Waiting is not passive; It is formative.

And the most difficult truth of all is this, God often allows us to live inside a story we don't yet understand because understanding too soon would limit what He can do later.

We want explanation.

God wants completion.

Miranda's life could not turn all at once until the *old obligations ended*, the *false attachments dissolved*, and the *internal losses healed enough* to receive something new without fear.

Waiting did not mean she was forgotten. It meant the work was still underway.

And most of that work was invisible.

WHY THE SIGNS COME IN CLUSTERS

When restoration finally shows itself, it rarely comes politely. It doesn't knock once and wait. It arrives **in clusters**. It sends multiple confirmations. There are usually multiple shifts and multiple moments that say the same thing from different directions.

Why?

Because after a long season of loss, one sign is not enough. God knows this. One answered prayer can be dismissed as coincidence. One breakthrough can be second-guessed. One open door can be feared as temporary, if you're not discerning, wise, careful.

But **five?** Eight? Ten confirmations in the same stretch of time? That is not Mercy trying to convince God. That is God convincing *you*. Clustered signs silence doubt without requiring explanation.

Miranda did not need someone to tell her she was restored. Her voice returned. Her burden lifted. Her companionship aligned. Her joy resurfaced.

Each sign reinforced the next and the next.

Voice alone might have felt fragile. Love alone might have felt risky. Freedom alone might have felt empty. But together? Together they formed **certainty**.

Clusters are how God speaks in His way, saying, **"This isn't temporary." "This isn't imagined." This is not man-made or man-orchestrated." "This isn't going to be taken back."**

When signs come back-to-back, it is often because the season you are leaving was long — and God is merciful enough to leave no room for doubt. It is up to you then to know how God talks. It is up to you to hear Him, see His signs, interpret those signs by help of the

Holy Spirit and recognize that your defining day could very well be approaching.

This is not God rushing. This is God revealing. The work was done slowly. The proof is delivered quickly. But when it happens, people often say, *"Everything changed overnight."*

It didn't. Everything appeared overnight. That is the defining day. Not the day the work began, not even the day the work finished, but the day the evidence finally spoke and spoke loudly enough to be believed.

THE MOMENT YOU KNEW

There is always a quiet moment, often unannounced, when knowing replaces hoping. It isn't loud. It isn't dramatic. It doesn't feel like fireworks; it just *is*..

Instead, it feels like settling. Being established, really and fully established, for the first time, ever.

But the God of all grace, who hath called us unto his eternal glory by Christ Jesus, after that ye have suffered a while, make you perfect, stablish, strengthen, settle you. (1 Peter 5:10)

For Miranda, it wasn't the proposal. I t wasn't the laughter, although that laughter was glorious. It wasn't even the return of her voice. It was the accumulation.

The realization that nothing in her life required her to brace herself anymore. That is

29

Peace. When you know that God has really got this, God has really got you; that is that Peace that defies understanding, that is Peace like a river.

No one needed managing. No one needed rescuing. No one needed enduring. She could simply **be**. That is often how you know, when vigilance and hyper vigilance leaves.

The moment you realize you are no longer scanning for the next blow. The moment your body relaxes before your mind catches up. The moment Peace shows up uninvited. It is the moment that all the things that pertain to your Peace show up--, both the things you knew about and perhaps had prayed about, as well as the things you knew nothing about and had never mentioned to the Lord. But He knew.

Defining days rarely announce themselves while they are happening. They reveal themselves afterward, when you realize something fundamental has shifted.

And once you see it, you cannot unsee it. The story has turned.

WHY GOD LET YOU DOUBT ALONG THE WAY

Doubt is not the enemy of faith, unexamined certainty is. God allows doubt because doubt keeps us honest. If everything were clear while we waited, we would confuse endurance with entitlement. We would mistake patience for leverage.

Doubt keeps us dependent.

Miranda could not map her future because certainty would have anchored her to outcomes that were not yet safe. Doubt prevented her from forcing resolution too early. It protected her from accepting substitutes. It kept her from believing the story was over when it was only incomplete.

God does not shy away; He knows the weaknesses of man. He works through doubt.

Doubt is often the space where humility grows and humility is the only soil where true restoration can take root.

Now faith is the substance of things hoped for, the evidence of things not seen.
(Hebrews 11:1)

Faith that has never wrestled becomes fragile. Faith that has survived uncertainty becomes grounded; it becomes strong faith. There are many kinds of faith, and we can grow our faith from no faith to weak faith, all the way to strong Faith in God.

The goal was never blind belief.

The goal was prepared belief and consistent faith. Faith is shown in a man and also to God by substance. What in the natural is showing God that you have faith in spiritual things? Your actions, your words, your own steadfastness. Your trust in Him. Your diligence and your courage to keep on another day and to keep on believing—those are some of the *substances* of Faith.

RECOGNIZING YOUR OWN DEFINING DAY

Most people expect a defining day to look obvious. They imagine announcements. They imagine applause. They imagine relief so dramatic it can't be mistaken.

But defining days are often quieter than expected. You don't always recognize them while they're happening. You recognize them in retrospect, when you realize how many things shifted without your effort. You may realize that things that you couldn't have shifted even if you tried have indeed moved out of the way. Finally. Joyfully.

Defining days rarely arrive while we are striving for them. They come when striving has finished its work and no longer governs us. This is not passivity, and it is not resignation; it is trust that has matured beyond urgency.

When we stop forcing outcomes, manipulating timing, people, and situations through human effort we create space for God to move. We create **alignment**. In that space, and in His Grace, God is no longer resisted. What He has prepared does not need to be chased. It arrives when we are no longer trying to prove readiness, but are willing to receive without strain. Many good things, many defining days do not come because we finally did enough, but because we finally stopped doing what was never required and got out of God's way.

One day about 20 years ago, as I was speaking to an audience I said, "And some of us are still trying to fix stuff we did 10 years ago, 20 years ago." At that time, I was speaking of the mistake, the error, the sin, I was not considering that some things we cannot fix ourselves, anyway. But now I see differently. God's defining days often arrive not when we try harder, but when we stop interfering with what He is doing for us and especially with what He has already finished.

A defining day is marked by **alignment**. **Alignment is not agreement with circumstances; it is agreement with God.** It is not a feeling, a vibration, or a technique. It is the quiet, deliberate choice to stand where God has already spoken, even when evidence has not yet caught up. Alignment means your words, posture, expectations, and your refusals all point in the same direction. You are no longer pulled by urgency or pushed by fear. You are not chasing outcomes or negotiating timelines. You are positioned both internally and externally, in a way that allows what God has finished to be revealed without distortion. Alignment does not force results; it removes resistance and *allows* results. When alignment is established, movement becomes orderly, waiting becomes intelligent, and the defining day arrives without needing to be summoned.

Conversations change. Resistance lifts. Outcomes converge. What once required explanation no longer does. You recognize your defining day not because you feel euphoric but because the story stops fighting you. When the work has been finished, striving loses its grip. And if you miss the day itself, don't worry. The fruit will make it known.

WHEN THE SIGNS DON'T ALL COME AT ONCE

Not every restoration arrives in a neat cluster. Sometimes the signs are staggered. Sometimes they are subtle, or incomplete.

This does not mean God is absent, It means the story is still unfolding. Clusters are Mercy for the weary, but staggered signs are training for discernment.

Some seasons teach you to trust the pattern rather than the timing. Some seasons ask you to live without punctuation. This is not punishment. It is preparation. A single sign can still be true, even if it is lonely.

Know this: when the full picture does arrive, you will recognize how each earlier sign was necessary.

THE FULLNESS OF FAITH

There is a difference between believing God *can* and believing God *will*. Most believers live somewhere in between. They believe God answers prayer, just not all of them. They believe God restores, just not completely. You may have heard the old folks praying or saying something about a portion of health, or what their portion is.

They believe God provides, and He provides only just enough. Though that is not the God I serve. I serve a God of More than Enough, El Shaddai.

But for those who believe partially, they have partial faith. Faith becomes careful. Measured. Reasonable. A sample here. A taste there. A crumb from the Master's table. Enough to survive, Enough to stay hopeful.

Enough to keep going. But not enough to expect fullness.

The fullness of faith comes later; and it comes quietly. It comes after disappointment has taught you discernment. After delay has taught you patience. After partial answers have taught you restraint. Then, one day, something shifts. You finally understand what the promises actually say. Not what you reduced them to in order to cope. Not what you spiritualized to avoid disappointment. But what they say.

And for the first time, you believe they are for you. Not in theory. Not symbolically. Not eventually. But fully, and fully for you, and now.

However, this is where many people hesitate. Because partial faith feels safer. They don't want to err and especially not on the side of pride or greed thinking they could have so much. Although Scripture says exceeding and abundant... more than we could ask or think.

Without ego, if we ever know who we are to God, then it being His good pleasure to bless us would not be a mystery at all. The delay, my friends, is development. God is developed, the plan is developed, we are formed and we are *becoming*.

If you expect little, you risk little. If you hope cautiously, you can explain away loss. If you only reach for crumbs, you never have to wrestle with abundance.

But fullness of faith is different. Fullness says, God does not tease with promises. God does not offer samples of what He never intends to give. God does not invite you to the table to starve politely.

Fullness of faith is not greed; it is agreement with what God already said. Agreement with what Christ already secured. Agreement with what delay never canceled.

When faith becomes full, you stop negotiating outcomes. You stop settling for proximity instead of participation. You stop confusing humility with hesitation.

You don't demand. You receive, not because you are worthy, but because He who promised is.

This kind of faith doesn't arrive early, it arrives after you have learned that crumbs were never the point, the entire table was always intended for you as soon as you developed in Wisdom, discretion and got into alignment.

When fullness comes, it doesn't shout. It settles. You realize you are no longer asking *if* God will come through, only *when* He will reveal what is already done.

That is fullness of faith. It's not just excitement, not presumption and not entitlement, but quiet, grounded confidence that all of what was promised belongs, in its time, to you.

By the time it arrives you are more excited that it arrived than what it is. You are more interested in that it arrived, that God is, more than God did it. It is the difference between desiring the natural or earthly wealth than the true riches. When your mind and eyes and heart are on the true riches, that is when it will arrive.

Yes, I'm tying it to value -- you cannot know the value of a thing until you KNOW what it is-- as well as what it is for, etc.

Look at this order: identity, then purpose, then value is placed. That's the order Scripture uses. The order is key. You cannot assign value before you understand identity. You cannot understand identity without knowing purpose. In biblical terms:

1. *What is it?* (identity / nature)

2. *What is it for?* (purpose / function)

3. *What is it worth?* (value/ stewardship)

Reverse the order and everything breaks. That is why misevaluation leads to misuse, and misuse leads to loss.

God waits for you to see this, and once you see it, you will see how it all connects. God does not release things to us early because early release often means the wrong valuation will be placed on a thing or person. Easy come, easy go is really a thing.

God is not into being esteemed lightly, nor does He expect that you will esteem what He places under your care or stewardship to be esteemed lightly. If you don't know what something *is*, you will either idolize it, or trivialize it. If you don't know what something *is for*, you will either exploit it, or waste it. So, God waits, not to withhold, but to protect both the gift *and* the receiver.

You cannot know the value of a thing until you know what it is, and what it is for. Until a thing is rightly understood, it cannot be rightly valued. What is not rightly valued cannot be safely released.

God allowed Adam to name the Creation before Adam was allowed to govern it. Identity came before authority. Understanding came before possession. Value followed recognition.

Value follows understanding. God releases according to understanding. God does not release what we admire simply because we admire or want it. He releases what we understand. Until we know what a thing is — and what it is for — we cannot know its true value.

This explains why crumbs came first and why fullness came later. It explains why defining days arrive only after long formation. It demonstrates why revelation feels sudden but is never premature. It also protects us from entitlement, impatience, and spiritualized greed which are all connected to pride.

Therefore, the wait now makes sense.

God releases according to understanding, not desire.

WHEN THE DEFINING DAY IS NOT GOOD

But when it is not all coming up roses, we have to look deeper.

God created the heavens and the Earth and He said it was good. But earlier there was darkness and void over the face of the deep. God creates; the enemy destroys. God creates, the enemy impersonates. God does it; the enemy counterfeits it. God makes perfect things and perfected things, heavens, Earth, sun, moon, stars, and everything within His Creation. The enemy comes to destroy. God speaks to create light; the enemy wants darkness. God is working toward defining a perfect day; the enemy? The opposite.

Therefore, we must know that the enemy will try to define your day, any day, or any night, with his own evil imaginations and not with the Word of God or by the *Will* of God.

So what do you do when the day that defines your day, week, month, season or year is not good? After all, not every defining day arrives as blessing.

Some arrive as **clarity**.

There are days when something does not resolve, but **reveals**. When a pattern escalates. When a truth surfaces. When an attempt is exposed. When a trajectory becomes undeniable.

Yet, t*his is the day it showed itself.*

God is not the author of confusion, darkness or evil. It may be allowed, but it is not of God. But the counterfeiter will try to trick anyone that he can and he will try to define your day before God can. This is why we command our days and nights because by default, if we do nothing, evil is waiting to take over.

There may come a day, and you've may have heard people say it, *I knew when I saw this that or the other*, or *I knew when this happened*, or *Ever since that happened, things have not been the same.*

Now the challenge is to make it thru and out of that day and continue believing on the Lord for the fine day that He has prepared for you.

THIS IS THE DAY

This is the day that the Lord has made, we will rejoice and be glad in it. Every morning new mercies.

Scripture is honest about this, when the Light shines on darkness, darkness must scatter. But we will see that darkness for what it is when God allows us to see it. Light does not only reveal good things. Light reveals things that must be confronted. Light reveals darkness that we must see.

Sometimes the Mercy is not in prevention, but He will teach our fingers to fight and our hands to do battle. It is difficult to fight if we cannot see. So, the sun arises on that defining day and what will be defined is: *Are you God's? Are you a warrior? Will you stand or will you flee?*

The defining day, in this sense, is not the day God *gave* something, it is the day God removed ambiguity. It is the day that God revealed something. It is the day that God revealed you---, to you.

Before that day, you might have minimized reality, explained away spiritual things that needed to be dealt with as coincidences. You may have just hoped things would improve on their own. You may have been fearful and had to get over so much fear. I know I have had to become courageous and very courageous.

After that day, you no longer wonder *what this is*. You cannot resist what you refuse to look at, to see, and to name. You cannot guard against what remains undefined. You cannot close a door that you pretend isn't open. You cannot close your own eyes and pretend the enemy doesn't see you.

A defining day is not always the day of fulfillment. Sometimes it is the day of **discernment**. Sometimes it is a day of resolve. I know that if I don't do this, who will? Sometimes it is a day of willingness to go into battle—whether you go or not, be willing because the Lord says He will fight our battles for us, but He doesn't say that we shouldn't be ready to go with.

A defining day could be the day when what was hidden becomes visible, and what was subtle becomes obvious. It could be the day that what was attempting to gain entrance is exposed. That day is not failure; that day is not the end. That day could be the very beginning. In the Beginning darkness was over the face of the Deep; but that was the beginning and not the end.

In Scripture, exposure often precedes deliverance. Recognition comes before authority. Naming comes before governance. How can you name a thing that you can't see or won't look at?

That applies to evil just as much as good.

Not every defining day brings what we hoped for. Some defining days bring what we needed to see, what we must see; and seeing clearly is often the beginning of protection. Some defining days do not resolve a story.

They expose it. And exposure, though painful, is Mercy.

Many have had days they mark because something crossed a line.

Recognition, even when painful, is still a form of Grace.

God didn't cause it, but didn't Job have, at least at first, a 'defining day'? His was marked as the beginning of woes as he suffered loss after loss. But then God steps in to **redefine** the day and make it a better day than the false day that tried to define a man's life.

A redefined 'day'? Yes, Miranda at 10 and beyond, up to Miranda as a grown and seasoned woman, and now, fully redeemed and restored to what her original estate that God intended from the beginning.

WHEN A FALSE DEFINING DAY TRIES TO CLAIM A LIFE

God does not cause destruction — but He does allow days that **expose** it.

Job had one of those days. In a single stretch of time, everything collapsed. Loss stacked on loss. Bad news followed bad news. That day did not come from God, but it *did* try to define Job. It attempted to declare: *This is who you are now. This is what your life will be like. This is where your story ends.*

But Scripture is careful; God did not author that day, and God did not allow it to have the final word. What followed was not immediate relief, but **redefinition**. God stepped in, not to explain Himself, but to reframe the story. The false defining day did not get to stand; God reclaimed the narrative.

False defining days are real, but they are not final. Many people can point to a day like that. A day when something began that should not have. A day when something escalated, or when something tried to enter and stay.

Miranda had such a day when she was ten. That day tried to define her life as loss, as premature responsibility, as a future narrowed too early. But that day was not the truth, it was an intrusion. God did not leave it unchallenged. Years later, God gave Miranda another defining day, not one of collapse, but one of convergence. Not one that took, but one that restored. The latter day did not erase the earlier one; it superseded it, outranking the false day. *When the Lord restored His people, we were like those who dream.*

This is how God works. God allows false defining days to reveal themselves, but He does not let them remain sovereign. It is according to your faith, it is according to your relationship with God as to how long this will take and if it will reverse in your favor. We please God with our faith and when He is pleased, He, in turn, pleases us.

He does not rush to override those days. If He is allowing something, He is using it. So, God waits until they have shown what they are. Then, in His time, He redefines. The later defining day does not pretend the earlier one didn't happen. It simply refuses to let it decide the meaning of a life. That is what redemption looks like. It is not denial; it is not amnesia; it is authority reclaimed.

Not every defining day is from God but every defining day God allows, He reserves the right to redefine. Some days try to define you falsely, and God answers those days with a truer one. So, let God be true and every man a liar.

The glory of this latter house shall be greater than of the former, saith the Lord of hosts: and in this place will I give peace, saith the Lord of hosts. (Haggai 2:9)

Why does that childhood or young adult day still loom large? Why does that crisis still feel like it tried to rename them? Why does the later restoration feel not just good, but corrective? Something bad happened, but it did not get the last word.

PRAYER: RENOUNCING THE FALSE DEFINING DAY

Father God, I acknowledge the day that tried to define me. I name it for what it was — an intrusion, not an identity.

I reject every meaning that day attempted to assign: fear, limitation, loss, distortion, and false authority.

I do not agree with what was spoken over me, decided about me, or attempted against me outside of Your will.

I receive Your Truth as final. I stand in what You have named me.

What You did not author, I do not enthrone.

In Jesus' Name. Amen.

STANDING WHEN YOU KNOW WHAT IS NOT YOURS

Discernment changes how you stand. Before discernment, you react. After discernment, you **resist**.

Now we visit discernment, hope, and faith again to know how to stand when you know what is trying to define you and not the real thing that God has for you, says you are, or is not what you're supposed to have.

This is the **stance chapter. It is about** how to stand *after* recognition, *before* fulfillment.

Once you know what is trying to define you, and you recognize that it is not from God, you stop arguing with it and stop internalizing it. You no longer ask whether it is fair, permanent, or deserved.

You ask only one question: *Is this the thing God has named me, or is this some other thing trying to name me?* That question steadies you.

Discernment does not immediately remove pressure, but it does remove **confusion** which is what weakens faith. When you know that what is pressing on you is not the real thing God has spoken, when you know it is an intrusion, a distortion, a false claim it is at that time that hope changes shape.

Hope stops being wishful. It becomes anchored. You are no longer hoping *something* will change. You are believing, even knowing that God's Word will stand. That is a different kind of hope.

Faith, at this stage, is not optimism. It is alignment. Faith says, *I will not agree with what is attempting to define me. I will not live as though this is final. I will not build my identity around a season God did not author.*

People can misunderstand faith when they think it is pretending that some false thing isn't happening. That is not faith. Faith is knowing it is happening—and knowing it does not have authority.

Standing in faith does not mean you feel strong. It means you refuse to concede meaning. You may still be under pressure. You may still be waiting. But you are no longer undecided about who you are, what you are called to, or what you are meant to have.

Discernment names the false thing. Hope keeps you oriented toward the true thing. Faith holds the line in between.

This is not passive waiting; this is standing with understanding. When you stand this way—without panic, without negotiation, without shrinking, you are already participating in the redefining work of God.

The false defining day only has power while it is believed. A person can playact within a false day and still believe the falsehoods of the day. Life is not playacting.

Once the lies and misspoken words and imaginations of the day are seen clearly, that day begins to unravel and lose its claim.

Dear Reader, you stand—not because the real defining day has arrived yet, but because you know it will. Not as a correction made in haste, but as a revelation made in fullness.

That is how you stand when you know what is trying to define you, and you know it is not the real thing God has spoken. When God said, **LET US MAKE MAN IN OUR OWN IMAGE AND LIKENESS,** man was already defined. Just as when He created the heavens and the Earth those things were already defined. It was the enemy who came in to redefine or to keep man and Creation from knowing who they are. Once identity is made, purpose and valuation follow.

THIS IS THE DAY THAT THE LORD HAS MADE

I will rejoice in be glad in the day that the Lord has made. Let's discuss what that day would normally look like and how we should ASK for that day or command that day in the position of prayer.

First, we need to clear away a common misunderstanding. *"This is the day that the LORD has made; we will rejoice and be glad in it."* This verse is not a command to feel happy about whatever happens today. It is not denial or playacting. It is not emotional override or toxic positivity. It is not pretending the day is good because it exists. Biblically, *"the day the LORD has made"* is not any day. It is a particular day.

It is a day God authors and anchors. A day God defines. A day God claims. Which means that most days are lived but the days that God has for us are **made**. We can then know that days are custom made for God's people. And then we must remember there is a counterfeiter loose in the Earth.

A day the Lord has made often looks ordinary on the surface. No fireworks, no announcements, no spiritual theatrics. But, internally, something is different. A God-made day usually includes alignment instead of friction. clarity instead of confusion, confirmation instead of striving, authority instead of anxiety. Externally, it may look like conversations landing differently, doors opening without force, resistance lifting without explanation, truth becoming undeniable. Sometimes, and very importantly, it looks like exposure before elevation.

Because a day the Lord makes is not always a day that *feels* good at first. It is a day that **becomes** true. That's why Scripture pairs it with rejoicing, not because the day is pleasant, but because the day is authored.

Should we ask for that day, or command it? We can position ourselves for a God-made day, even a defining day by commanding the morning, commanding the day, even commanding the night before. Clearing the environment; setting the atmosphere. We'd do it for date night, so why not for a defining day?

We can ask for God's defining day, agree with God's timing, refuse and reject false defining days, and stand until the true one arrives.

The posture is not, "God, do this now." No, we do not dare command God. No, it is, "Father, **I will not accept a counterfeit.**

That is warfare.

That is alignment.

That is mature faith.

PRAYER: FOR THE DAY THE LORD HAS MADE

Lord,
I ask You to make my days to be the days that
bears Your authorship.

I reject every false defining day.

I reject every day that claims authority You
did not give it.

I ask for the day You have made:
the day of clarity,
the day of Truth,
the day when what You have finished
is revealed without striving.

I will not force timing.
I will not accept substitutes.
I will stand. Let the days that You have
authored arrive.

In every day that you have made, I will
rejoice and be glad in it, because You have
made it and graciously given it,

In Jesus' Name. Amen.

Th

GIVE US THIS DAY

When the Disciples asked Jesus to show them how to pray, He taught them what we know as the Lord's Prayer. The line, Give Us This Day can be a prayer unto itself. Give Us the Day You Made for us.... and not the enemy's "day."

The petition, Give us this day, is bigger than provision. We've almost all been trained to hear, *"Give us this day our daily bread"* as a prayer about sustenance. And it is.

But it is not *only* that.

"Give us this day" is a request before bread is mentioned. Which means the *day* matters. Days are not promised, so being given days is a blessing. The *authorship of the day* matters. and not every day is assumed to be neutral.

Jesus did not teach us to pray, *Bless* whatever day shows up. This is reminiscent of how we humans sometimes devise our own plans and then ask the Lord to bless it. Can He? Should He? Why didn't we ask before we did the 'thing'?

Jesus taught us to pray, Give us this day. That implies selection. Days aren't promised—and not every day is from the Lord. Scripture knows this; it is clear that there are evil days, there are days of adversity, there are days when the enemy seeks advantage. Paul even says, *"Redeeming the time, because the days are evil."* Which means some days are contested. As far as the enemy is concerned, any day can be up for grabs and that is why his evil agents can be up all night, or at least in the wee hours attempting to steal days or program them for evil. Some days attempt to define, some days attempt to steal authority.

So, when we pray *"Give us this day,"* we are not being naïve. We are asking God to author, govern, and assign the day with our own agreement with Heaven and not just wishful thinking. This is why we say when we pray. We desire the day to agree with us, not the enemy, nor circumstance, nor trauma, nor our own bloodline, or generational or family history.

Lord, give us the day You made for us. Lord, let me live inside a day You made. And in that I will rejoice and be glad. Amen. If I have to ask each day, I will. If I have to pray about it each night, or in the wee hours or just before dawn in a commanding prayer, I will. I will agree with Heaven so the day the Lord has made will present in my life. If God is loading us daily with benefits and each morning there are tender mercies, then a "made" day, made by the Lord, is a real thing and I want that.

In the Beginning God created all kinds of good things over six days. God created Time, therefore He has created days. And after God created all that, He created, He said, "IT IS GOOD." So, it stands to reason that the days the Lord has created for me are GOOD.

Also, if the Sabbath is the Lord's day, then that means in a week, if we give Him that day, He will give us the other 6. Six, the number of man.

PRAYER: GIVE US THIS DAY

Our Father,

Give us the day You have prepared: the day that carries Your Will, Your timing, and Your Truth.

We reject every false day that seeks to name us redefine us to the negative, or claim authority You did not give it.

We receive the day You have made and when it comes, we will rejoice, because it is Yours and you gave it to us.

In Jesus' Name. Amen.

The old language about *"more good days than bad days"* sounds hopeful, but it's actually passive. It assumes days just *happen to us* and we tally them afterward. That is not how dominion works.

Scripture treats days like territory; therefore, we should too. You don't just *hope* the territory is peaceful; you walk into the Promised Land, and you govern it. So, the goal is not "I hope today is a good day." The declaration and goal is that this day will not govern me; I will govern it.

Some folks end up Fighting for Every Day. Many Believers feel like every day is a battle, that's the life and legacy that has been given and left to them. But now that we are in Christ, things should be different. Every day is a battle if we're trying to win days instead of establish rule.

Winning requires effort every time, over and over again. Rule requires establishment once, then maintenance. If you have to fight for a good day every morning, it usually means boundaries were never set, authority was never established, false definitions were never permanently rejected. So, the enemy keeps testing, not because you're weak but because nothing told him to stop trying..

That's where your declarative prayers come in. Choose the Day as a habit and not as a struggle. Choosing the day becomes *regular* when three things are settled.

1. **Identity Is No Longer Negotiable.** The day stops fighting you when it knows *you are not up for redefinition or re-identification.*

Once you have clarity about who you are and what you belong to, many days lose their leverage automatically. This is why false defining days are so dangerous. They try to destabilize identity, so every future day is contested.

2. **Value Is Correctly Assigned**. When you know what truly matters, fewer things get permission to affect the day. Most bad days aren't bad because of events. They're bad because too much was given value. Once value is settled delays don't hijack the day, resistance doesn't define the day, disappointment doesn't own the day. Now you're in authority and you don't need to fight what you've already demoted.

3. **Authority Is Exercised Early, Not Reactively**. There is a difference between governing the day, and reacting to or

responding to the day. The earlier authority is exercised, the less effort is required later.

This is why Scripture talks about commanding the morning, redeeming the time, restoring the years, and standing therefore.

You don't wait to see what the day does before you decide who rules it. Of a fact, you already know what the enemy will do in a day if he is allowed: steal, kill, and destroy. So, why wait? It's the same game plan every day.

Make this your habit so that false defining days have been named and rejected. Your identity in Christ is settled. Your value is clarified. And, your authority is exercised confidently. At that point, most days don't need a fight. They fall into alignment because order has been established.

The goal is not to have more good days than bad days, the goal is to live from a place where days no longer compete for authority. When identity is settled, value is clear, and authority is established, choosing the day stops being a battle and becomes a posture.

You don't fight for a good day forever. You do fight, however, until rule is established.

Make sure that you are in Christ and that you are ruling. When those annoying enemies that have been nagging you for seasons and years see that you have stepped into dominion authority – it's a new day for real. They will leave you alone.

Look at Psalm 91. It is the *settled place* where you abide in your proper authority. Psalm 91 is where the day stops competing for authority. Psalm 91 is a governing psalm.

> He who dwells in the secret place of the Most High shall abide under the shadow of the Almighty.

The language is not reactive. It is positional. This psalm is not written to someone scrambling through bad days. It is written to someone who has chosen where they live. When you dwell, you are not visiting. You are not passing through. You are not checking conditions. You have taken up residence. People choose to place their residence in places of peace and order.

Psalm 91 does not promise the absence of danger, but it does promise authority over it. The snare may exist. The terror may pass through. The arrow may fly. But none of them get to decide the meaning of the day (or the night).

Why?

Because the person in Psalm 91 is not managing days, they are abiding. This is where choosing the day becomes normal instead of exhausting.

You are no longer waking up asking, *What kind of day will this be?* You are waking up from a place that already knows the answer. position is settled. Psalm 91 is what happens when identity is no longer negotiable, value is no longer confused, authority is no longer reactive. It is the difference between fighting for peace, and living where peace governs. The writer isn't trying to survive the day. They are ruling from shelter.

When you dwell, you don't fight for a good day. You don't tally good days versus bad days. You don't negotiate with fear each morning. You live from a place where days are received, governed, and released. Psalm 91 is not about escaping life. It's about out ruling and outlasting false authority.

DAYS ARE PRECIOUS

So teach us to number our days,
that we may gain a heart of wisdom.
(Psalm 90:12)

Teach us to number our days is far deeper than time management or mortality awareness. The word **number** there is doing much heavier work than we usually allow it to do.

This is not a prayer about counting days. It is a prayer about discernment. If "number" only meant arithmetic, it would not produce *Wisdom*. But Scripture ties numbering directly to understanding, ordering, and weight. To number a thing in Scripture is to recognize its place, understand its role, assign its weight, and relate it correctly to the whole.

In other words, to number a day is to know what kind of day it is.

Numbering vs. Enduring. Most people endure days. Maybe they don't want to get out of bed, dread for the day ahead, traffic, work, same ole, same ole. They survive them. React to them. Recover from them. But they do not number them.

Numbering a day means you don't let every day claim the same authority. Some days are formative, instructional, resisting, transitional. As some days are defining, revelatory, corrective, or God-authored.

Lord, teach me to see the difference, in the Name of Jesus. Wisdom comes from knowing the difference.

If you treat every day as equal, you will overreact to small days, underestimate significant ones, exhaust yourself fighting days that require endurance, miss days that require recognition. So, the prayer is not, *Help me survive time*. It is, *Help me discern meaning*. God creates days; we govern within them. *Numbering* a day is how we remove false authority from time.

Numbering is about value, not quantity. Looking again at identity leading to purpose and that leading to value, ask: What is this day *for*? What does it require of me? What should it *not* be allowed to define?

When a day is not numbered, it can steal weight it doesn't deserve claim authority it doesn't have, masquerade as destiny when it is only weather. Numbering strips false authority.

When you can discern, *"You are a day of resistance, not revelation." "You are a day of endurance, not conclusion." "You are a day that passes through, not a day that names me."* That is Wisdom.

Numbering days and dominion connects directly to commanding the morning and governing the day. You cannot govern what you have not discerned, identified, named, called. Numbering is discernment applied to time. It is how dominion becomes intelligent instead of reactive.

A numbered day is received correctly, governed calmly and released without residue. An unnumbered day lingers. It follows you. It tries to define you long after it has passed.

Psalm 90:12 is the *inner mechanism* behind false defining days, true defining days, waiting and recognizing when God reveals meaning. It explains why some days mark us and others don't. Wisdom is not knowing how many days you have left, it is knowing which days matter, and how, as well as which days don't, and which days must not be allowed to speak.

To number our days is not to count them, but to discern them. It is to recognize which days are formative, which are passing, and which must not be allowed to define a life.

Wisdom is not gained by enduring time, but by understanding it. Numbering a day is how we remove authority from time and return it to God.

"Teach us to number our days" is not the prayer of someone afraid of dying, it is the prayer of someone who refuses to be misdefined by time.

Discernment becomes habit, and use, not effort. It is about accuracy more than urgency.

INTRINSIC VS EXTRINSIC VALUE

Intrinsic Value, Extrinsic Value, and True Riches

Much of our confusion about faith comes from confusing value. We live in a world trained to recognize extrinsic value, value assigned by outside forces.

- Titles.
- Money.
- Status.
- Visibility.
- Approval.

Extrinsic value depends on who is looking and what they reward. It rises and falls with markets, moods, and opinions.

It is never stable.

...for the Lord seeth not as man seeth; for man looketh on the outward appearance, but the Lord looketh on the heart. (1 Samiel 16:7B)

Intrinsic value is different. Intrinsic value exists before recognition, before applause or reward. It is value because of *what a thing is*, not what it produces.

A human life has intrinsic value. Truth has intrinsic value. Faithfulness has intrinsic value. Character has intrinsic value. These listed do not become valuable only when someone notices them. They are valuable whether or not anyone does.

This distinction matters, especially when we talk about true riches, we will see that true riches are durable riches, eternal; their value will never diminish. Jesus never condemned wealth. He redefined riches. True riches are not what you accumulate; true riches are bestowed upon you. True riches cannot be taken from you. Ever.

Peace that survives loss, Wisdom earned through waiting, discernment shaped by disappointment, and faith refined rather than inflated are all true riches. They are intrinsically rich realities.

They do not sparkle. They do not advertise. They do not need validation; they simply *are*.

And yet, they endure.

Extrinsic riches can be added or removed overnight. It is why Jesus said don't store up uncertain riches. That was sound advice that He could give after passing the temptation by the devil in the wilderness where He was offered the kingdoms of the world.

Intrinsic riches are formed slowly and revealed carefully. That is why God often allows us to live without what looks like visible reward for long stretches of time. Of course, true riches are not visible. But God does not randomly or quickly download these blessings, not because He is withholding, but because His vetting process is thorough.

He is building something so precious that no one else can give it; no one else has it and cannot duplicate it. It is true riches and they cannot be corrupted or stolen.

This is where fullness of faith becomes clear. Fullness of faith is not believing you will get *things*. It is believing God is forming true riches in you. Just the awe of knowing that you are being prepared as a vessel of honor to even contain such eternal wealth should make any of us submit wholeheartedly to the process. He is not done until the work is complete; therefore, if you have the fullness of faith you will avail yourself to what the Lord is doing in you.

But if you only think of the outward and what you look like to others that is all you may want or think is available to you. You may think that just being adorned on the outside is enough. Maybe if you look successful, or if the people at church think you are holy, that's enough. That is Pharisaical thinking. Just wanting crumbs for adornment is extrinsic thinking. God looks on the inside, He cares what you look like on the outside, but He doesn't weigh outer appearances to decide on true riches, intrinsic value or whether or when to deposit true riches.

Crumb-seekers assume scarcity. They accept partial access. They manage disappointment by lowering expectation. But true riches are not distributed in samples; they are inherited, and inheritance requires time.

The irony is that by the time true riches are revealed outwardly, they have already been secured inwardly.

Which is why defining days often feel dreamlike. For example, if the lack of finances is the problem and you are having stress because of that, by the time the defining day comes when God answers the money issue, true riches have already been deposited and taken effect, so you have Peace like a river FIRST, then the natural solution shows itself. Having the Peace in advance of the extrinsic thing makes you love God and focus on the Peace because it is more of a relief than the money. That is why people with prospered souls and intrinsic riches behave differently than people who are just money grubbing and looking for their own solutions for outward appearances.

The world sees the result, but you recognize the formation within yourself. What others call sudden favor, you know as long obedience with strong faith and a refining process that you have been through to make you who you now are.

What others call luck, you recognize as alignment. God is Father, and you've come into the Kingdom as a little child. This is what the Word instructs.

What others envy externally was forged internally You are more impressed with God than with things and stuff--, that's a prospered soul. Nothing was manipulated or created, it was *formed* within and then refined, redefined, and then transformed. Like everything that He made in the Beginning, when He saw that it was good; He blessed it. When you submitted to God's refining and transformation to *become*, then God blessed you. Your inner man changed and your outer man represented to the world.

True riches are not loud, but they are weighty. They do not rush but they do arrive whole.

When God finally allows extrinsic evidence to match intrinsic reality, you understand something quietly profound: there is nothing missing, nothing broken; nothing was wasted. nothing was delayed unnecessarily. Nothing that mattered was lacking. That is the difference between value assigned by the world and value revealed by God.

One fades.

The other endures.

When all things finally work together, true riches are not something you chase. They are something you recognize, because they were being formed in you all along. When you get here, your defining day is most likely to appear. God will not bring it too early and though it may seem to tarry for you, it will not be too late. Although your flesh wants it now your spirit and soul have to go through changes to be ready for blessings. Like a dental procedure, sometimes you have to get numb which many don't believe they want in order for the transformation of that tooth.

When your intrinsic value rises, when your soul prospers and your soul prosperity reaches the right levels, that is when those things that we see as having extrinsic value will show up. But it is the man who sees that the things of intrinsic value are actually more enduring and of higher worth. This is what is happening behind the scenes of waiting for that defining day.

When you need me versus. *when you want me* is a line from Nanny McPhee that stays with people long after they forget the plot of the movie. *"When you need me but do not want me, I must stay. When you want me but no longer need me, I have to go."*

That line describes maturity, not preference.

In the early stages of faith, we *need* God and we need Him desperately, but we may not always want Him because working through our *"stuff"* is usually very uncomfortable.

Most want the comfort and the relief God offers but not the discipline and requirements of God. We want answers. We want rescue; we want ease, but we may resist *formation.* We resist restraint. We resist refining, most of us believing that there's nothing wrong with me, *right*? We resist timing because we want it now.

So, God stays. He stays through the waiting. He stays through the discipline. He stays through the silence, not because it's pleasant, but because it's necessary.

Later, something changes.

We begin to want God — not just His outcomes, but His presence. Not just His help, but His ways. We want His comfort, His Peace, His Love. He has put a new heart in us, a heart of flesh and now we are more relational, with Him as well as with others. He has put His Spirit in us and now we are more alive. We are moving, and breathing and having *being*. We love the Lord more than anything. And paradoxically, by then, we no longer *need* Him in the same panicked way. Not because we are independent but because we are formed.

That is when God releases what once had to be withheld. This is where fullness of faith lives. When faith is no longer driven by desperation, God can trust us with abundance. When we stop grabbing crumbs to survive, we are ready for the entire table.

True riches require a heart that wants God not just what God can fix. When that shift happens, the season changes. That change is not because God has left, but because He has finished what that season required.

When the Lord endows you with true riches, things like the fruit of the Spirit to include Peace that passes all understanding, shows up. This causes you to know that He is the Lord. God said more than once in the Bible... you will know that I am the Lord.

When the right value is placed on the right thing, in the right way, that is when it appears. What God reveals appears only when the right value has been rightly placed. Right value precedes right appearance. When value is aligned, appearance follows. Did the Son of Man appear before the fullness of Time? No. God does not rush.

When value is finally aligned, what was finished quietly is revealed openly. When the right value is placed on the right thing, the right way, it appears. In right alignment, what God will do in you, through you, and for you will be like a dream.

TRUSTING GOD AGAIN AFTER YOU'VE BEEN RIGHT BEFORE

Sometimes, faith looks different *after* a defining day than it did before one.

There is a quiet danger after a defining day. It is the temptation to assume future outcomes will follow the same or familiar patterns. God does not repeat Himself to prove consistency. He reveals Himself to deepen trust.

He that hath my commandments, and keepeth them, he it is that loveth me: and he that loveth me shall be loved of my Father, and I will love him, and will manifest myself to him. (John 14:21)

But faith is not prediction. Past faithfulness is not a contract; it is a witness. Because God reveals Himself one way in one case doesn't mean He will do the same again the same way. Why would He do that? God has more ways of being God and if He just keeps showing Himself the same way every time, how will be ever get to know Him? This is one of the reasons why the testimony of others is so powerful; they are revealing God to us as God has revealed Himself to them.

The challenge is not believing God *can* do it again. The challenge is believing He will do it differently and still be God.

Faith that has survived one defining day does not require replication, it requires more Faith because God is ***all that***, and He can do what He pleases, as He pleases. The assurance we have is that He loves us and there is no shadow of turning in Him. Now your faith has to grow, it has to expand. This is why we have testimonies in the Bible; what He did for others He can do for you. But knowing God, and especially knowing Him by His attributes and by discernment and help of the Holy Spirit in prayer, we may know what attribute of God to call on in prayer. Still, He will show up and He will show up as God, not by our rigid, limited understanding but by the wondrous awe that He is. And in that we will know that

He is the Lord. He doesn't always show up subtly or symbolically, but it will be clear to us. Jesus promised this kind of revealing.

I will not leave you comfortless: I will come to you. (John 14)

God does not always explain the process. But He does keep His Word about presence. There are moments when God answers simply because He said He would show Himself.

These moments are not earned; They are declared. And when they come, they carry a different weight than blessing alone.

They carry recognition.

You don't just feel relieved; you know.

This was not coincidence, timing, nor was it human orchestration. This was God, stepping into the open. THEN YOU WILL KNOW THAT I AM THE LORD

When God stops working quietly and He begins to show Himself. No, He hasn't been absent; it is just time for Him to be recognized.

Throughout Scripture, God repeats a phrase again and again: *"Then you will know that I am the LORD.* " This is not arrogance; it is revelation. God reveals Himself because relationship requires recognition.

There are seasons when faith is built in the dark. There are times when God asks for trust without explanation. But then there are moments when God steps forward, unmistakably, and says,

This was Me.

WHEN THE DEFINING DAY BELONGS TO SOMEONE ELSE

One of the tests of maturity is witnessing restoration that is not yours. You can believe in defining days in theory, but will you behave yourself well when you are standing beside someone else's or listening to their overcoming testimony?

When you are listening to their joy, seeing their burdens lifted and hearing how their story resolves, will you behave yourself? What if your story is still suspended?

Rejoice with them that do rejoice, and weep with them that weep.(Romans 12:15)

God is looking at your heart; what will He see? Listening to someone else's testimony may depend on a different kind of Grace. Or, it may show that your heart needs cleansing.

Miranda's defining day did not belong to me. Whether she was a friend or a stranger, it brought me great joy. Her testimony and the Blood of the Lamb, her overcoming showed me God. The Lord desires to reveal Himself to us; I saw God in this. I saw what happened in Miranda's life as a witness, as a testimony.

In Christ there is no jealousy or covetousness, therefore I rejoiced with her as we are told to rejoice with those who rejoice. I celebrated the risen Christ as if He were walking a bright sunny street and we were in company with Him, fully revealed. I know that what He will do for one, He will do for others. I am one of those others. A young woman I know would say when people around her were getting blessed that she was fine because maybe tomorrow would be her day.

That's where I live in my heart. If there are works of the flesh and envy, that just means that the refining and the becoming is not even close and the manifestation of joy, peace, and full deliverance will take that much longer.

A cleansed heart requires you to celebrate without comparison. It requires you to rejoice without resentment, to acknowledge

God's faithfulness without demanding immediate proof in your own life.

> Blessed are the pure in heart: for they shall see God. (Matthew 5:8)

Blessed are the pure in heart for they shall see God, and we know from our verse in John 14:21 if God is revealing Himself to those that keep His commandments, that is another way of saying that they shall see God.

People can falter here if they think God is taking too long or that God is blessing others and not them. That is jealousy, envy, covetousness; that must stop. When outcomes are uneven, when timing is uneven, when Grace and favor seem unfair without explanation, the one without soul prosperity will act up. This will repel true riches, and it will repel blessings and delay the divine defining day.

Jesus said that when you've done something unto the least, you've done it unto Him. I can see that corollary a different way: If the Lord has done this for anyone, whether I know them or not, whether they are my friend or not, whether or not they are my relative, then it's all good. It's all joy; He has done it unto me. Maybe tomorrow will be my day. Maybe it's right now as I'm listening to their testimony.

Why? Because the same anointing that delivered them can also deliver me.

Why? How?

Because I saw it. Because I heard it. Because He **revealed** Himself in the Earth realm and I was either there, or adjacent to the miracle, the deliverance. Because I saw it; I saw Him at His revealing, and that is true riches.

Someone else's defining day is not evidence of your delay, it is evidence that God finishes stories; the Great Advocate completes cases, and we win every time. It is evidence that if He finishes their story and their case, He has not forgotten yours. It is evidence of how near He is. And the same anointing that delivered them, is in the midst of this meeting – or even a television or online program, and it can also deliver me. In the Name of Jesus, Amen.

Think about this: If you are in a meeting with 100,000 people and 99,999 got delivered, won't you be happy for them? If not, you may be the only one who doesn't get a defining day that day because of your heart. God is looking at that heart. *Right?* Right.

Sometimes the lesson is not, *Look what God did for them,* it is, *Look what God is doing right now. Jesus Christ is in the midst of us. Amen.*

Nor will people say, 'Look, here it is,' or There it is.' For you see, the kingdom of God is in your midst. (Luke 17:21 BSB)

WHAT TO DO WHILE YOU'RE WAITING AGAIN

Waiting does not end permanently. It changes shape. After a defining day, waiting becomes quieter but it does not disappear. There is only waiting if God is still working on your case and He is moving you from faith to faith and strength to strength, else you will be in a season of rest and Hallelujah for that.

You wait with memory now. You wait with history. You wait knowing what resolution feels like and what revelation is like. If you are waiting for another level of deliverance or another defining day, this kind of waiting asks different things of you. It asks you not to rush closure or to force meaning. It says, *Do not rewrite the past to make the present easier.* Waiting again is rarely empty; It is filled with memory. When memory is God-focused, it becomes one of faith's greatest allies.

Scripture does not treat memory as nostalgia. It treats memory as **witness**. Again and again, God calls His people to remember, not because they are prone to sentiment, but because man is prone to forget and prone to fear.

God-focused memory does not replay the pain. It recalls the **faithfulness**. It recalls the goodness of God. It recalls the power of God. It recalls the Love and kindness of God. It does not rehearse how long the night was; it remembers that morning came and God is the one who brought it.

This is the difference between memory that weakens faith and memory that strengthens it. Memory can build up your faith, or it can build up your flesh. The carnal man says, "Look what I did, what I accomplished. Look what I defeated."

God did that, not you.

When memory centers on loss, it breeds anxiety. When memory centers on God, it builds confidence. That is one of the reasons why waiting again is not the same. Yes, because God can reveal Himself in a new way this time, as we discussed. But it is different because you should have stronger faith now and that stronger faith should be in God, not in yourself. Not in mankind in general, and not in medicine, banks, the lottery, or other modalities that may have been used to attempt to correct whatever matter you were trying to correct.

Before, faith was hope without evidence. Now, faith is hope **with history**. Memory becomes a quiet anchor. And that anchor will grow you into a person of faith and great faith, or it can dismantle your belief in God, depending on how you remember it and how you tell it.

They overcame by the Blood of the Lamb and the Word of their testimony. The Word in your testimony will make you an overcomer. Amen.

When that Word is both in you and coming out of your mouth via your testimony it makes you steadfast and able to stand. You remember: *He did it before. He did it rightly.*

He did it mighty. He did it in His time. God delivered me. Amen.

God-focused memory does not rush the future. It steadies the present. It keeps faith from collapsing into desperation and prevents patience from turning into resignation.

Waiting again is not starting over, it is standing on remembrance and trusting that the God who revealed Himself before has not changed but He is able to reveal Himself again another way. Logically, if Jehovah Saba'oth was revealed in your last deliverance, wouldn't Jehovah Saba'oth have done all that God in that attribute would have done? Then, another attribute of God will show next time, say, Jehovah Jireh, unless you keep needing the same deliverance over and over.

Waiting again is not regression; it is relational and it is continuation. God is still Father and you are still His child (son). The danger is trying to relive the same defining day, instead of letting it inform you. God does not repeat moments for emotional reinforcement; He builds upon them. Waiting becomes less about outcome and more about posture.

STANDING THEREFORE

One morning, some years ago, right after I had awakened, I got the urge or inspiration to stand on my bed. So, I stood there for some seconds or minutes -- I don't know how long. Then within myself or out loud, I asked, "What am I standing here for?"

Within myself I heard the Spirit of God speak, "YOU ARE STANDING THEREFORE."

This was positional language, not instructional language. It indicated that something has already been decided. resisted, or concluded. "Therefore" only comes *after* something.

"Therefore" has Biblical weight. In Scripture, *therefore* always points back to **truth already established**. Because this is true, therefore stand. Because this has been decided, therefore hold. Because this cannot move, therefore remain. Standing is not anticipation there, it is response.

I was not standing to make something happen, I was standing because something already had.

That's why the moment had force without explanation. It was given without explanation because some truths are meant to be inhabited, not analyzed. I didn't know and really didn't need to know *what* I was standing against—not just yet. I needed to know how to stand when I did. I needed to learn how to obey. That's formation.

That moment wasn't about trying to claim authority, it was about authority that I was recognizing. Standing was not in defense, or in desperation or fear. It was not in performance or show. No one else was present. Standing was in conclusion.

Standing is the posture of someone who knows: *This does not get to define me. This has already been addressed. I am not waiting to see what happens next.*

So, Dear Reader, stand until your defining day is from the Lord. Stand, therefore.

PRAYER Standing for the Lord's Defining Day

Lord,
I yield my timeline to Yours.

I choose understanding over
impatience,
agreement over striving,
and truth over appearances.

I stand against every false definition
and wait for what You have finished
to be revealed in Your time.

I trust that what You author
will arrive whole, rightly valued,
and unmistakably Yours.

I am ready. I am not early. I am not
late.

I am aligned.

In Jesus' Name. Amen.

WHEN YOU ARE THE SIGN FOR SOMEONE ELSE

Eventually, you may realize something humbling. Your defining day was never meant to end with you. It was meant for someone watching your life the way I watched Miranda's. Your defining day was meant for others. It was meant for testimony and for praise.

Someone is measuring hope by your survival. Someone is drawing courage from your endurance. Someone is waiting to see if restoration is possible — and they are watching *you*.

You do not have to announce your story. You do not have to frame it as testimony.

Your peace speaks. Your steadiness speaks. Your lack of bitterness speaks.

Sometimes the sign is not what God does **for** you, but what He has done *in* you.

When that realization settles, the question changes again. Not *"When will my next defining day come?* Instead, it may be, *"Who might need to see me standing in the meantime?"*

That is not pressure; it is purpose.

ALL THINGS WORKING TOGETHER

And we know that all things work together
for good to them that love God, to them who
are the called according to his purpose.
(Romans 8:28)

Some outcomes are impressive. They
are impossible to attribute to anyone but God.
There is a difference between something going
well and something coming together so
precisely that no single person, plan, or effort
can claim credit.

This is where the phrase *"all things
working together"* stops being inspirational
language and becomes **evidence**. This is what
I was seeing when I saw sign after sign and
believed my defining day had come or was
approaching and very near. Still, I would reject
not one sign, indication, or blessing from God,
but these things made me believe that I was

like the prophet looking at the clouds in the sky to see the weather, and long-desired rain was approaching.

Whether it culminated into the defining day or not, I know that no one thing could have caused this. My own effort over many days, weeks, months or years couldn't have done this. It was not by my effort or persistence. It was not even faith, by itself.

When all things are working together, praise God. When many variables converge and timelines align we know the Lord is at work. When many doors open and close in the correct sequence it is the Lord's doing.

This is how God removes doubt without argument. He does not defend Himself. He outworks every alternative explanation.

When restoration comes this way, you don't have to convince yourself it was God.

You eliminate everything else first, knowing that no human could have timed it. No manipulation could have coordinated it. No shortcut could have preserved its integrity.

Only God could have woven loss, delay, restraint, silence, endurance, release, and joy into the same outcome, and brought them into view together. That is not randomness. That is authorship. And when you see it, you stop asking *if* God heard. You understand that He was listening the entire time. The defining day is not proof that God suddenly acted. It is proof that God was always at work and finally chose to let you see it.

In my case, I saw the Lord moving on my behalf, but then I saw Miranda's defining day and to me that was also a sign for me. Hallelujah!

LIVING AFTER THE DEFINING DAY

The defining day does not freeze life in perfection. Bills still come. People still disappoint. Bodies still age, but something fundamental changes.

You stop negotiating with despair.

You stop explaining yourself to fear.

You stop wondering whether God is capable because capability has already been demonstrated. The defining day does not remove struggle; it reorders it.

You carry proof now. Real, revealed proof. Memory becomes an anchor. History becomes a witness. Testimony is inspiration. Faith is strengthened. The Lord has revealed Himself and it is life-changing, life-renewing, and life-giving. Where hopes had slept or died, they are now awakened and resurrected.

When new challenges appear, and they will, you are no longer guessing who God is. He has revealed Himself to you. If you are wise you will recall that God has many attributes and just because you see one facet of Him, doesn't mean that that is all there is. This is how people get stuck. I saw the Lord, He was here, so I will sit right here so I can see Him again and have this same experience all over again. There is so much more to God even though what He showed you was probably much for a mere mortal.

You have seen what He can assemble. God can create, He can refine, He can renew--, there is nothing that God cannot do. Nothing is impossible with Him.

You have lived through His timing. Now you understand some things about God, but you don't know everything about God. Keep learning, keep seeking Him, keep spending time with Him. Keep walking with the Lord.

All this changes how you wait the next time. That changes how you see things and discern next time. That changes how you handle yourself and the situation next time. You are more grounded and you are fully persuaded of who God is, that God is and that He is a rewarder of those who diligently seek Him.

But without faith it is impossible to please him: for he that cometh to God must believe that he is, and that he is a rewarder of them that diligently seek him.
(Hebrews 11:6)

The defining day does not eliminate questions. It answers them. *Is this story worth trusting? Does God hear prayers? Does God answer prayers? Does God see you? Does God know you and love you? Can you trust God?* Yes, and more than ever. Amen.

Once those yes answers come, you are no longer the same person who entered the waiting.

THE LORD'S PERFECT DEFINING DAY

Scripture tells us something quietly astonishing, *When the fullness of time had come, God sent forth His Son.*

Jesus did not arrive early. He did not arrive late. He arrived on a defining day.

For generations, humanity waited — often without knowing what it was waiting for. They expected deliverance, but misunderstood the form. They longed for rescue, but misjudged the nature of the Rescuer. Simeon and Anna were two individuals who eagerly awaited and prayed for the redemption of Israel (Luke 2:22-40).

The promise existed long before the recognition. God did not release His greatest gift until the world was prepared to recognize its value.

Even when Jesus came, not everyone recognized Him. But enough recognized Him to enthrone Him. Enough followed Him. Enough saw more than a carpenter, more than a teacher, more than a miracle-worker. Enough realized who He was--, enough to make Him go viral.

To enthrone Christ was to place the right value on the right Person, the right way. Until that valuation was possible, the gift was not released. This is not because God waits for human permission., it is because revelation requires readiness.

Jesus Himself said that pearls are not cast before those who cannot value them. Not because the pearls are fragile, but because misunderstanding leads to desecration.

The Lord's defining day came when Heaven and Earth aligned. It came when prophecy, history, language, culture, and longing converged. The world had learned enough suffering to recognize salvation.

Enough law to recognize grace. Enough emptiness to recognize fullness.

So, Jesus came, not as spectacle, not for conquest, but as the Word in flesh, as Truth, embodied. This was God's perfect defining day.

This was not the beginning of the plan, but it was the revealing of it. In the same way, God does not release the fullness of promise into a life until the promise can be rightly valued.

We often think delay is about worthiness. It is not. It is about understanding.

Until we know what something *is*, until we know what it is *for*, we cannot value it rightly. What cannot be rightly valued cannot be safely enthroned. This is why God waits, not to withhold. But to ensure that when the gift arrives, it is not diminished.

Jesus was not sent as an experiment. He was sent as fulfillment. The Lord's defining day teaches us this: God reveals Himself when revelation will be received as revelation not novelty, not utility, not leverage.

When the heart is finally able to say, without fear or negotiation: *This is who You are. This is what You are worth.* That is when defining days arrive. Full, but not rushed, and not random.

All the days of Creation are defining days. In Genesis, God doesn't create in a blur. He creates in days. In each day does three defining things: God speaks. Something is separated, ordered, or named, and then God declares it, **Good**. That is the anatomy of a defining day. So, if God can do that for a whole planet and universe, there is no end to what He can do for you. God speaks; what must be separated, ordered or named as it concerns you? Then let it be, and let God declare it as **Good**. Afterward God will bless what He calls, ***Good***.

A defining day is not just when something appears, it is when meaning is assigned. It is when order is established and that thing becomes *like God.*

Light is not merely created; it is separated from darkness; who can do that, but God? Waters are not just present; they are divided and bounded. Who can divide water from water? Only God. Life is not just formed; it is blessed and given purpose.

Each day suppresses chaos and entropy. Each day establishes order, sets jurisdiction. Each day closes with evaluation. Creation shows us the *first pattern*: God defines reality one day at a time, and once defined, it holds.

Creation shows us that a defining day does not need to be repeated; it is permanent. Light didn't need to be re-created. The heavens didn't need to be re-ordered. Once defined, the definition stood.

That explains why later defining days in our lives often feel *sudden*. *That is because God didn't have to scramble to prepare what we needed;* the work was already done. The order was already set. The meaning was already decided. The day simply revealed it.

Every day of Creation was a defining day because something permanent was established. God defines reality by days, not moments.

God delivered the heavens. He delivered the Earth. He fed mankind before He even formed him. Deliverance is the children's bread; what man would have children and not have provision for them? Deliverance was a matter of pre-provision, not rescue after failure. Seed-bearing plants and fruit trees were already in place before Adam took his first breath. Provision preceded presence.

The Lamb was slain before the foundation of the world.

God does not wait for crisis to act. He does not react; He anticipates. Creation is not God improvising a world and then fixing problems as they arise. It is God establishing *deliverance as this means that* later defining days are not anomalies. They are echoes of Genesis. So, God can deliver you from anything and everything that He delivered the Heavens and the Earth from in Genesis. And even more.

THE DAYSTAR

We have also a more sure word of prophecy;
whereunto ye do well that ye take heed, as
unto a light that shineth in a dark
place, until the day dawn, and
the day star arise in your hearts: (2 Peter 1:19)

The Daystar is about illumination from within, The above Scripture speaks of a light that does not rise in the sky first, but in the heart. The Daystar is not an external sign you chase. It is an internal awakening. This is important, because defining days are often recognized **after** something has already changed within us. Before the circumstances align, before the evidence appears, before the day is publicly named, the Daystar arises.

The heart sees what the eyes have not yet confirmed. This is how faith matures, not by waiting for proof, but by receiving illumination.

The Daystar does not shout. It does not rush. It does not compete with darkness. It simply rises and once it does, everything is seen differently. False defining days lose their authority. Waiting loses its confusion. Standing becomes natural instead of forced.

Because when the Daystar has risen in the heart, you no longer need the day to tell you who God is. You already know.

The outward defining day may still be ahead, but the inward one has already occurred. That is Mercy; God does not leave us in darkness while we wait. He gives light enough to stand, light enough to discern, and light enough to hope without anxiety.

This is why the Daystar matters.

It is the quiet assurance that the morning is real, even while the night still lingers. When the Lord's defining day finally arrives, it does not feel foreign; it feels familiar. Light that breaks the horizon is the same light that rose in the heart first.

The Daystar rises in the heart before the day is revealed in time.

Every defining day has a center. It is not the event, the outcome, or the timing; it is Christ.

The Daystar does not rise only once, nor only in the Heavens; He rises in the heart, and from there He governs what is revealed in time. What appears outwardly has already taken shape inwardly. Illumination precedes manifestation. This is why defining days are recognized, not chased. Jesus is the star of every day because He is the light by which days are seen and understood. He is the Light that scatters darkness. When the Daystar has already arisen within our own hearts, no defining day arrives as a surprise, it arrives as confirmation.

Every defining day bears witness to the same light—Christ, already risen within.

IT IS THE LORD'S DOING — AND IT IS MARVELOUS

There are moments when the correct response is not merely understanding; it is **marveling**. Scripture does not always invite us to explain God. Sometimes it invites us to stop and look.

"This is the LORD's doing; it is marvelous in our eyes."

Marveling is not childish wonder. It is mature recognition. It is what happens when the mind reaches the edge of explanation and the heart finally catches up.

God did not design us only to obey Him, trust Him, or wait on Him. He designed us to **see Him**. And He is a marvel.

The heavens declare His glory. The sky proclaims the work of His hands.

Creation itself does not argue God's existence; it displays it. And in the same way, there are seasons of our lives that become

display windows. When our own defining days are for others to see. For others to just look, not because we are prideful, but we are trying our very best, as His Creation to declare his glory and His mighty works. It is not because we are special, but because God chooses to reveal Himself through outcomes that cannot be explained any other way.

The heavens declare the glory of God; and the firmament sheweth his handywork.

Day unto day uttereth speech, and night unto night sheweth knowledge. (Psalm 19:1-2)

God does not hide His handiwork; the Heavens declare the glory of God. shall we not do the same so the rocks don't have to cry out? He signs it. He arranges things so precisely, so completely, so beautifully, that the only honest response left is wonder.

Not relief. Not pride. Not even gratitude alone. Wonder and awe.

Creation is simply **being what it was made to be,** and in doing so, it testifies.

That's important. This kind of glory is not reactive. It is inherent.

It doesn't argue. It doesn't persuade. It doesn't call attention to itself. It declares by existing in order.

Two kinds of witnesses and they are both marveling witnesses. Psalm 19 shows us e*nduring Glory. The heavens declare the glory of God; the skies proclaim the work of His hands.* This is glory as echo. Glory as resonance. Glory as continuance. Nothing (new) is "happening," yet everything is speaking.

It's the aftermath of Creation still testifying long after the act itself. It is still testifying because it is alive. What God creates lives, and it remains, and it marvels and it speaks and it testifies. Amen.

God went viral before anyone else. Following are a short list of works from Scripture that caused people to marvel then and that still provoke marveling now. These aren't minor wonders; they are enduring, repeat-told acts that refuse to fade.

Works of God That Have Always Provoked Marveling:

1. **Creation**. God spoke, and what did not exist *existed*. The Heavens still declare His Glory because Creation never stopped testifying. People have never moved past this marvel.

2. **The Flood and the Preservation of Life.** This was Divine Judgment and Mercy in the same act. The world was reset, yet life was preserved through obedience and covenant. The scale alone still overwhelms humankind.

3. **The Exodus (Red Sea Deliverance).** God did not remove the enemy; He divided reality. A sea became a road. Slaves became a nation. Scripture repeatedly returns to this moment as *the* defining act of deliverance. God proved that just as in Creation He can still divide the waters from the waters; **He is the Lord.**

4. **Manna in the Wilderness**. Daily provision with no storage, no hoarding, no manipulation. God fed a nation in a place where food could not exist, and stopped when the season ended. People

still marvel at provision that cannot be engineered.

5. **The Giving of the Law at Sinai**. Fire, sound, boundaries, and holiness made visible. God didn't just rescue a people, He revealed His nature. The weight of Sinai still shapes theology, morality, and reverence.

6. **The Incarnation (God Taking on Flesh).** .Eternity entered time. The Creator submitted to creation. This is perhaps the most *incomprehensible* marvel of all, and the one that never stops being contemplated.

7. **The Miracles of Jesus**. The blind saw. The lame walked. The dead rose. Not as spectacle, but as restoration. People didn't marvel because miracles happened, but because they happened rightly.

8. **The Resurrection of Jesus.** Death was defeated. This single act reordered history, hope, and Eternity. Nothing in Scripture is returned to

more often, because nothing surpassed it.

9. **The Sending of the Holy Spirit (Pentecost).** God did not stay distant. He indwelt His people. Languages, courage, authority, and conviction erupted—and the Church was born. This marvel is still unfolding.

Marveling continues when the work continues to hold. Every one of these glorious acts still holds.

Sometimes God does not act, He doesn't have to; He is simply recognized. *The heavens declare His glory* not because He is intervening, but because His order remains. Creation bears witness without effort. It speaks without words. It looks like a regular day; but it is so much more. It declares without urgency, and those with discernment see it, hear it, sense it, feel it, know it.

God's Glory is not always revealed through action, often, it is revealed through endurance. Through order that remains. Through Truth that does not need to be defended. The Heavens declare because they were made correctly, and that correctness still speaks.

Glory that follows God doesn't need to arrive, not if God was *ever* there. This is not about intervention Glory; it is about authorship Glory. It's not about what God just did, it is about what God established that is still standing.

Thy throne, O God, is for ever and ever: the sceptre of thy kingdom is a right sceptre
(Psalm 45:6)

When something is truly good, repetition is not tedious, it is natural. We repeat what delights us. We revisit what satisfies us. We do not grow weary of what is whole. Creation does not declare God's Glory once and then move on; it keeps singing because nothing has diminished its wonder. The song does not need updating. The Truth has not expired. What God established was good, and goodness does not exhaust itself. So the heavens keep declaring, the skies keep proclaiming, and the Earth keeps bearing witness--, and so should we, because what was done was done well.

Creation repeats the song because the goodness has not worn off and it never will. It will last forever.

And that's Glory.

…and they rest not day and night, saying, Holy, holy, holy, Lord God Almighty, which was, and is, and is to come. (Revelations 4:8b)

24/7 -- it never stops. Around the Throne, the cry never stops. *Holy, holy, holy.* Not because something new keeps happening, but because holiness does not diminish. It is not consumed by familiarity. The nearness does not dull it; the repetition does not exhaust it. The closer the gaze, the deeper the recognition. Eternity does not move past holiness; it abides in it. So, the cry continues, but because it is massive, expansive, infinite. There is always more to see in what is already complete.

The song never stops because the wonder never runs out. This is enduring Glory. It is forever and forevermore.

Creation keeps singing. Heaven keeps declaring, because **goodness, once seen, invites return.**

This is why defining days matter.

They are not about our success. They are not about our timing. They are not even about our faith getting it right. They are about God being **seen**. God wants to be recognized. He deserves to be recognized; He deserves all the glory, honor, and praise.

When you marvel at God, you stop reducing Him to outcomes and you deepen your relationship with Him. You stop managing Him with expectations. You stop shrinking Him to fit your spiritual lack of knowledge or your fear.

Marvel restores scale. It reminds you who you are dealing with.

When you have lived long enough, waited long enough, endured long enough, you realize something quietly profound:

God did not just answer your prayer; He revealed Himself.

Then you realize that divine defining day, as great as it was, was never the point; the **revelation** was.

So, if you find yourself standing in a moment you cannot explain where too much has aligned, where too much has healed, where too much has resolved at once, Do not rush past it. Do not overanalyze it.

Stand still. Stand, therefore.

Look.

Let yourself marvel.

Because *this* is the LORD's doing.

And it is, indeed, marvelous.

AMEN.

I seal these words decrees, declarations and prayers across every dimension and timeline, past, present, and future, to infinity, in the Name of Jesus.

I seal them with the Blood of Jesus and the Holy Spirit of Promise.

Any retaliation against this author, the reader or anyone who prays these prayers, makes these decrees and declarations at any time, let that retaliation backfire on the head of the perpetrator to infinity, and without Mercy, in the Name of Jesus.

Dear Reader

Thank you for acquiring and reading this book, **ONE DEFINING DAY** : *When Dreams Come True*

Shalom,

Dr. Marlene Miles

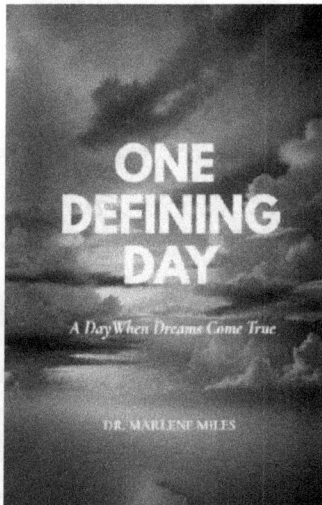

Prayerbooks by this author

There are some books that are only prayers. You just open up the book and pray.

Prayers Against Barrenness: *For Success in Business and Life*

Fruit of the Womb: *Prayers Against Barrenness*

Beauty Curses, *Warfare Prayers Against*
https://a.co/d/5Xlc20M

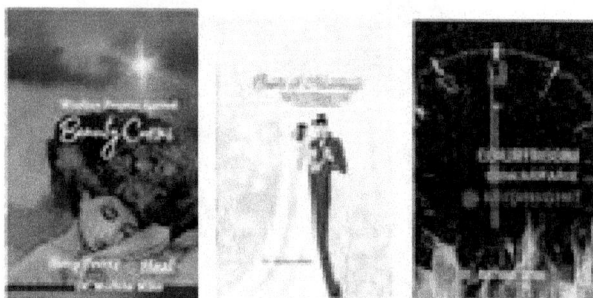

Courts of Marriage: Prayers for Marriage in the Courts of Heaven *(prayerbook)*
https://a.co/d/cNAdgAq

Courtroom Warfare @ Midnight
(prayerbook) https://a.co/d/5fc7Qdp

Demonic Cobwebs *(prayerbook)*
https://a.co/d/fp9Oa2H

Every Evil Bird https://a.co/d/hF1kh1O

Gates of Thanksgiving

Spirits of Death, Hell & the Grave, Pass Over Me and My House

Throne of Grace: Courtroom Prayer

Warfare Prayer Against Poverty
https://a.co/d/bZ611Yu

Prayer Books by this Author

Prayer Manuals

FAKE FRIENDS: *Prayers Against Betrayers*

HOLIDAY WARFARE Prayer Manual (humorous) Surviving Family Gatherings All Year Long (without catching a case)

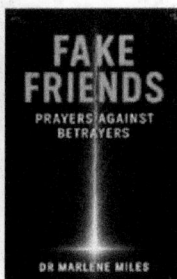

SOUL TIE Prayer Manual (The) Part of a 3-part series including a workbook.

MAD at DADDY Prayer Manual – part of a 3-part series including a workbook.

Healing the Sibling & Relative Wound Prayer Manual

Healing the Father-Son Wound Prayer Manual

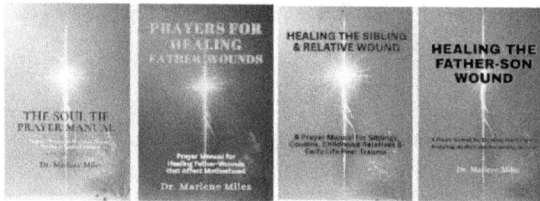

Prayers Against Barrenness: *For Success in Business and Life*

Breaking Curses of the Mother Prayer Manual

Other books by this author

Abundance of Jesus (The)
https://a.co/d/5gHJVed

AK: The Adventures of the Agape Kid

Already Married in the Spirit: *Why You May Not Be Married in the Natural*

AMONG SOME THIEVES
https://a.co/d/dkYT4ZV

Ancestral Powers

Anti-Marriage, *The Spirit of*

Backstabbers https://a.co/d/gi8iBxf

Barrenness, *Prayers Against*
https://a.co/d/feUltIs

Battlefield of Marriage, *The*

Beware of the Dog: Prayers Against Dogs in the Dream.

Bless Your Food: *Let the Dining Table be Undefiled* https://a.co/d/6oPMRDv

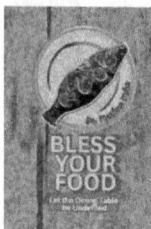

Blindsided: *Has the Old Man Bewitched You?* https://a.co/d/5O2fLLR

Break Free from Collective Captivity

Broken Spirits & Dry Bones

By Means of a Whorish Father

Caged Life: Get Out Alive! https://a.co/d/bwPbksX

Casting Down Imaginations

Christ of God (The) 3-book series

Christ of God, Box Set, includes all three books

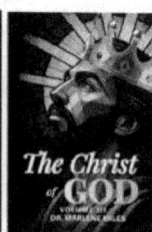

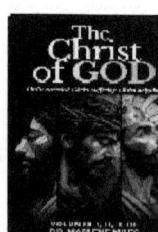

Churchzilla, The Wanna-Be, Supposed-to-be Bride of Christ
https://a.co/d/eAf5j3x

Collateral Damage: *When What Happened Spiritually Was Your Fault*

Demonic Cobwebs (prayerbook)

Demonic Time Bombs

Demons Hate Questions

Devil Loves Trauma, *The*

Devil Weapons: Unforgiveness, Bitterness,...

The Devourers: Thieves of Darkness 2

Do Not Swear by the Moon

Don't Refuse Me, Lord (4 book series)

https://a.co/d/idP34LG

Dream Defilement

The Emptiers: *Thieves of Darkness, 1*
https://a.co/d/5I4n5mc

Evil Touch

Failed Assignment

Fantasy Spirit Spouse
https://a.co/d/hW7oYbX

FAT Demons (The): *Breaking Demonic Curses* https://a.co/d/4kP8wV1

The Fold (5-book series)

- The Fold (Book 1)
- Name Your Seed (Book 2)
- The Poor Attitudes of Money (3)
- Do Not Orphan Your Seed (4)
- For the Sake of the Gospel (5)
- My Sowing Journal

Gang Ups: Touch Not God's Anointed

Gathered: No Longer Scattered
https://a.co/d/1i5DPIX

Getting Rid of Evil Spiritual Food

https://a.co/d/i2L3WYQ

got HEALING? Verses for Life

got LOVE? Verses for Life
https://a.co/d/8seXHPd

got HOPE? Verses for Life

got money? https://a.co/d/g2av41N

Has My Soul Been Sold?
https://a.co/d/dyB8hhA

Here Come the Horns: *Skilled to Destroy*
https://a.co/d/cZiNnkP

Hidden Sins: Hidden Iniquity

https://a.co/d/4Mth0wa

How to Dental Assist

How to Dental Assist2: Be Productive, Not Wasteful

How to STOP Being a Blind Witch or Warlock

I Take It Back

Irresistible: Jesus' Triumphal Entry
https://a.co/d/dO9IfEC

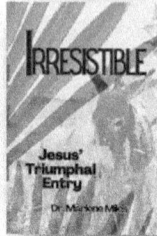

Legacy

Let Me Have A Dollar's Worth
https://a.co/d/h8F8XgE

Level the Playing Field

Living for the NOW of God

Lose My Location
https://a.co/d/crD6mV9

Love Breaks Your Heart

Mad At Daddy: Healing Father-Wounds
that Affect Motherhood (book, workbook
& prayer manual)

Made Perfect In Love

Mammon https://a.co/d/29yhMG7

Man Safari, *The*

Marriage Ed. Rules of Engagement & Marriage

Made Perfect in Love

Money Hunters: Beware of Those

Money on the Altar https://a.co/d/4EqJ2Nr

Mulberry Tree, *The* https://a.co/d/9nR9rRb

Motherboard (The)- *Soul Prosperity Series*

Name Your Seed

Occupy: *Until I Return* https://a.co/d/bZ7ztUy

Opponent, Adversary, or Enemy?: Fight The Right Battle with the Right Weapons

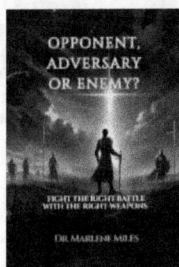

Plantation Souls

Players Gonna Play

Portals: Shut the Front Door: Prayers to Close Evil Portals.

Power Money: Nine Times the Tithe

https://a.co/d/gRt41gy

The Power to Get Wealth
https://a.co/d/e4ub4Ov

Powers Above

The Robe, Part 1, The Lessons of Joseph

The Robe, Part II, The Lessons of Joseph

Seasons of Grief

Seasons of Siege: GOD IS COMING

Seasons of Waiting

Seasons of War

Second Marriage, Third--, *Any Marriage*

https://a.co/d/6m6GN4N

Seducing Spirits: Idolatry & Whoredoms

https://a.co/d/4Jq4WEs

Shut the Front Door: *Prayers to Close Portals* https://a.co/d/cH4TWJj

Sift You Like Wheat

Six Men Short: What Has Happened to all the Men?

SLAVE

Sleep Afflictions & Really Bad Dreams https://a.co/d/f8sDmgv

Soul Prosperity soul prosperity series 3

https://a.co/d/5p8YvCN

Soul Ties: How Soul Ties Form, and How To Break Them (book, workbook & prayer manual)

Souls Captivity soul prosperity series 2

The Spirit of Anti-Marriage

The Spirit of Poverty https://a.co/d/abV2o2e

Spiritual Thieves https://a.co/d/eqPPz33

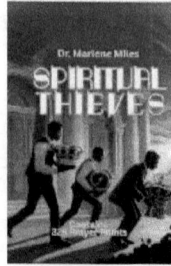

StarStruck- Triangular Power series.

SUNBLOCK- Triangular Power series.

The Swallowers: *Thieves of Darkness*, 3

Take It Back

This Is NOT That: How to Keep Demons from Coming at You

Time Is of the Essence

Too Many Wives: *Why You Have Lady Problems*

Tormenting Spirits
https://a.co/d/dAogEJf

Toxic Souls

Triangular Power *(series),* Powers Above, SUNBLOCK, Do Not Swear by the Moon, STARSTRUCK

Unbreak My Heart: *Don't Let Me Die*

Uncontested Doom

Unguarded Hours, *The*

Unseen Life, *The* (forthcoming)

Upgrade: How to Get Out of Survival Mode Toxic Souls (Book 2 of series) , Legacy (Book 3 of series)

The Wasters: *Thieves of Darkness,* Bk 2
https://a.co/d/bUvI9Jo

What Have You to Declare? What Do You Have With You from Where You've Been?

When I Was A Child, *I Prayed As a Child*

When the Devourer is Rebuked

https://a.co/d/1HVv8oq

When the Table Is set Against You

WTH? Get Me Out of This Hell
https://a.co/d/a7WBGJh

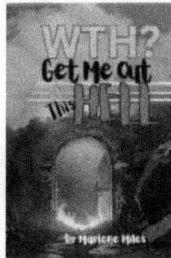

The Wilderness Romance *(series)* This series is about conducting a Godly relationship and marriage with someone who is a Wilderness person. It is about how to recognize it and navigate through it. These books are about how not to get caught up in such.

- *The Social Wilderness*
- *The Sexual Wilderness*
- *The Spiritual Wilderness*

Other Series

The Fold (a series on Godly finances)
https://a.co/d/4hz3unj

Soul Prosperity Series https://a.co/d/bz2M42q

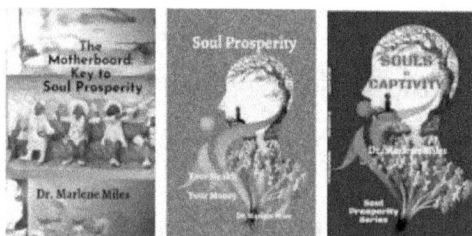

Spirit Spouse books

https://a.co/d/9VehDSo

https://a.co/d/97sKOwm

Battlefield of Marriage, The

https://a.co/d/eUDzizO

Players Gonna Play

https://a.co/d/2hzGw3N

Sent Spirit Spouse (can someone send you a spirit spouse? This book is not yet released.)

Matters of the Heart, Made Perfect in Love https://a.co/d/7OMQW3O , Love Breaks Your Heart https://a.co/d/4KvuQLZ, Unbreak My Heart https://a.co/d/84ceZ6M Broken Spirits & Dry Bones https://a.co/d/e6iedNP

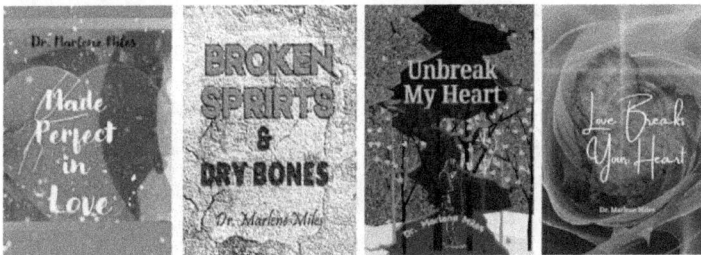

Thieves of Darkness series

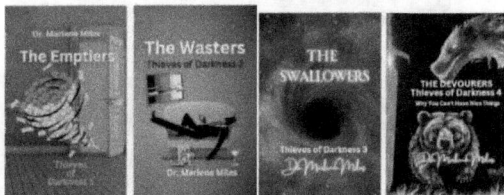

The Emptiers https://a.co/d/heioOdO

The Wasters https://a.co/d/5TG1iNQ

The Swallowers https://a.co/d/1jWhM6G

The Devourers: Why We Can't Have Nice Things https://a.co/d/87Tejbf

Spiritual Thieves

Triangular Powers https://a.co/d/aUCjAWC

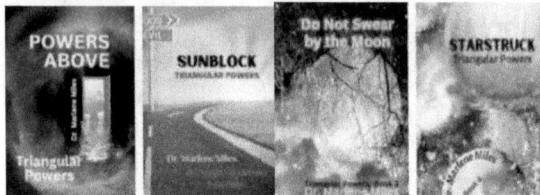

Upgrade (series) *How to Get Out of Survival Mode* https://a.co/d/aTERhXO

We Get Along, Right? Compatibility for Couples – (book & workbook)

www.ingramcontent.com/pod-product-compliance
Lightning Source LLC
LaVergne TN
LVHW052028080426
835513LV00018B/2230